No Butts About It

How to Want to Stop Smoking

John Randolph Parker

Copyright © 1985 by John Randolph Parker
All rights reserved

Second Printing
1989

Cover Design and Illustrations by Yvonne B. Taylor
Typesetting by Jackie Albert

Printed by
McNaughton & Gunn, Inc.
Ann Arbor, Michigan

A  Book

Published by
Johmax Books, Inc.
Larchmont, NY 10538

ISBN 0-912095-00-8

TO MARCY

and

To the memory of
BOB HOFFMAN

PROCEED WITH CAUTION

This book is not a gimmick. Its purpose is to help *you* stop smoking. Only by reading from the first page through the last will you benefit fully from the intended impact I believe it can have upon you. Therefore, I urge you not to "peek" at the last chapter or read ahead in any way. Each chapter sets the mood for what is disclosed in the next one. To jump ahead could dilute or destroy the very purpose of this book. It doesn't take long to read. So, again, I urge you to read it, one page at a time. By doing this, I believe that, soon, you will be able to say, "Parker's done it!" But, most importantly, I truly believe that you will be able to say, *"I've* done it!" — finally!

stupid adj.,

Lacking ordinary activity and keenness of mind; slow thinking.

Ponder this . . .

Each morning, you start your day by ambling out to your car and proceed to do the following.
1. Open hood.
2. Take a pail of sand and pour into the crankcase . . . drop a few pebbles into it for old time's sake.
3. Close hood.

Turn ignition key and *hope* car will start, because you know that what you've just done didn't do the engine a damn bit of good.

5. Repeat this process 365 days a year — each day *hoping* the ol' engine will do its job. Have car washed frequently to give it that ol' spit 'n polish look.

If that's not stupid, what is!? But, that is just what heavy smokers do — each day. Only smokers are *really* stupid, because a person who abuses his or her car can always get a new one. But, with excruciatingly few exceptions, it's very difficult to purchase a new heart, pancreas, tongue, lung, esophagus, or any number of other rather important parts of the human machine.

Think about it.

idiot n.,

An utterly foolish or senseless person.

WARNING: The Surgeon General Has Determined That Cigarette Smoking *Is* Dangerous to Your Health.

One must assume that the Surgeon General is fairly well thought of in the medical field. In all his wisdom, he has said that (since 1964! so make that Surgeons General), smoking cigarettes not only can be a dangerous thing to do, but, in fact, *is*. This warning is on every pack of cigarettes. Ever wonder why beer can be advertised on television and cigarettes no longer can? *That's* how dangerous they're supposed to be!

subliminal   adj.,

Existing or operating below the threshold of consciousness.

Ponder *this* . . .

Each morning you stop by a smoke shop and pick up your daily quota of smoke. It doesn't come in the familiar, very smart looking, 3½" x 2" package. Instead, your daily ration comes to you in a lightweight container about the size of a water cooler jug. It's clear, so you can see the smoke. You simply use a plastic tube to suck the smoke through and into your body during the day.

Question: Would you *really* take a jug-full of smoke into your body (the only one you'll ever have) if you could actually see all the smoke you were about to inhale *before* you did it?

Now really.

I am owner of the sphere,
Of the seven stars and the solar year,
Of Caesar's hand, and Plato's brain,
Of Lord Christ's heart, and Shakespeare's strain.

R. Waldo Emerson

Gather your family, friends and loved ones 'round and read the above to them. Then *try* to tell yourself that there is no way you can stop smoking cigarettes *right now!* (You don't even have to remind yourself that an average cigarette contains not a handful, but several *armsful* of chemicals!)

TABLE OF CONTENTS

	PAGE
PREFACE	1
INTRODUCTION	3
SMOKING IS A WAY OF LIFE	9
DON'T GET OLDER, GET BETTER	17
TAIN'T FUNNY, McGEE	23
TREADMILLS ARE HABIT FORMING	31
THE SMOKER'S HALL OF FAME	35
CRUTCHES I HAVE KNOWN	49
HOW TO WANT TO	61
AFTERWORD	68

PREFACE

At age 51, the author has smoked a total of 424,000 cigarettes (minimum) during his lifetime. That comes to 21,200 packs. That comes to about 20 miles! At an average of 50 cents per pack, he spent a cool $10,600 — doing something that, during much of the time, was *officially* dangerous to his health.

Parker is an "expert" at kicking the smoking habit. He quit scores of times. He figures he could have smoked 21 miles worth of cigarettes if he hadn't stopped so many times. He stopped three times following sessions with a hypnotherapist. And began again. Following a heart attack, he continued to smoke at least two packs a day. Having a heart attack, he says, tends to make one a mite nervous and smoking helps to relax you.

He continued to be a heavy smoker until one day, four years ago, he decided to stop for good. He hasn't smoked during the past four years and *knows* he never will again. What follows is his unique treatment of the subject of smoking, written in an effort to help others to stop.

The reader will probably find his or her own smoking history reflected in what Parker has to say. This refreshing account of a smoker who decided four years ago that "the time had come" is often funny and entertaining and occasionally pathetic. All of which are adjectives that aptly describe the smoking process, he says.

Whether you are a smoker who has tried to stop and failed, or are a smoker who has never attempted to kick the habit, this book is for you — if you *NEVER* want to smoke another cigarette.

Most books and articles on stopping smoking conclude that a person must *want* to stop. By the time you finish reading this book, you will know *how* to want to.

INTRODUCTION

The simple act of purchasing this book is a clear indication that you smoke enough to know that you will be better off if you never smoke again. There is a very real possibility that you have already tried to stop—many times. "I can stop smoking anytime; I've done it a thousand times," is the old chestnut heavy smokers have kidded about over the years.

I will put my past stopping-and-starting-again record up against anybody's. Until I stopped smoking four years ago, I experienced just about every good and bad experience heavy smokers fall heir to. During most of the many years I smoked two or more packs a day, I wanted to stop. I did not want to be a cigarette smoker. I did stop, many times, for varying lengths of time. I stopped smoking anywhere from the too-familiar couple of hours to as long as a year and a half. The latter resulted from a bet of a case of scotch. (Something's counter-productive there, wouldn't you say?) The bet was for a year; I stayed off the habit for an extra six months. To this day, I can't remember why I resumed smoking after so long a time. (I once met a lady who stopped for nine years! She was back on the weed and she, too, couldn't remember why.)

But I do know that while I *wanted* to stop, I didn't know *how* to really want to. (During that year and a half I was off the weed, a day didn't go by that I didn't want to be back *on* the weed.) Now I do and I sincerely hope that what I have to say in this book will show you the *how* of wanting to. From experience (far too much experience, frankly), I know how much many of you truly want to stop smoking. I know that you have genuinely agonized over your inability to become a non-smoker. Moreover, I know that many of you are frightened of your prospects should you continue to smoke. Ideally, you wish the habit would "go away." Or, more likely, that the much-publicized dangers would cease to exist.

Every heavy smoker's fantasy is that, somehow, someone will suddenly announce that the ever increasing weight of evidence has been wrong and that smoking is, after all, not harmful in any way. But fantasy has little to do with the real world. The experts say that smoking will continue to cause preventable illnesses. Unfortunately, everything we've heard about the ills of smoking seems to be all too true.

As long as we live we will continue to read and hear about famous people or personal acquaintances, or even those closest to us, dying or being crippled and excessive smoking being given as a reason why. Obviously, smoking is here to stay. My aim here is to help to assure that *you* are here to stay for your fully allotted span of time—in the best possible health.

There's a lot of help out there. Each year, on a November day, The National Cancer Society sponsors the *Great American Smokeout*. The long and short of this exercise is that the National Cancer Society encourages smokers to give their smoking habit a 24-hour rest. I *never* participated. Most years that the *Smokeout* has been with us, I wasn't even aware that the big day had arrived. By the time I read about it in the newspaper or heard about it on radio or TV, I was already half way through a pack of cigarettes. (Sure as shootin', by the way, we are inevitably heading for a *Great American Drinkdown* in this country.)

There are television specials aimed at encouraging smokers to become non-smokers. There are by now omnipresent signs in public places thanking one and all for not smoking. There are a few books that treat the subject of stopping — anywhere from an entire book describing how to chew a special gum that can help, to processes of stopping that take days or weeks until that final day of cessation.

Of the books, articles, television specials, gum, prayer —you name it—the best method I have found to help one stop with the greatest ease is hypnotherapy. It has been my experience that physiological and psychological cravings that drive you up walls do not stop when you read the books, watch the TV programs or whatever. But I've batted 1,000 with hypnotheraphy. Following each of my three visits to one-to-one or one-to-group approaches, I have ended each session free of any of the usual withdrawal symptoms. The days following these visits were cigarette free and, importantly, I didn't even think of smoking.

Sadly, however, there were emotional experiences that occurred weeks or months after such visits that caused me to return to nicotine for solace. The books, etc., leave too much to chance, I believe, but the hypnotherapy route seems to me to have very real, helpful merits, *if* you want to stop in the first place and really know *how* to want to.

But, of course, whether you read the books, chew the gum, see the TV shows, or have the therapist count down from 10 to one, you're on your own afterwards. It's *lonely* out there, isn't it?

I have attempted throughout this book to tell it like it is. If you want to read statistics about what can happen to smokers, I suggest that you look elsewhere—there are plenty of statistics to be had in the other books. My purpose—and the primary aim of this book—is to *immerse* you in the subject of smoking, without getting you bogged down in details that will not help you to stop smoking one damn bit. They haven't helped yet, have they?

Please, read the book through, cover to cover. I've tried to make it educational, informational and entertaining, in and of itself. In short, I hope you find it a good read, as well as providing you with the beacon that you have been searching for—until now, in vain. As you progress through the various chapters, I believe that you will slowly begin the mental process of making the big decision. Special pages are provided throughout that will enable you to pause and take stock of yourself—to *think*. All of this will help to prepare you for the life you already know can be enjoyed to the fullest—if only you STOP!

I believe that you can stop smoking forever as a result of reading this book. Most other books written on the subject (surprisingly few in number) and various organizations that have been created to reach the same goal call for a few days or weeks of preparation before the actual cessation of smoking. These methods are valuable, I guess, and might help smokers give up the weed, often forever. I simply believe that lengthy preparation is not necessary. I believe that this book, for you, can work—as painlessly and as intelligently as humanly possible.

You now begin the immersion. God's speed!

John Randolph Parker
Larchmont, NY
January, 1985

**Tobacco Is Brown and Firm
And Fully Packed**

SMOKING IS A WAY OF LIFE

Not unlike drinkers, there is a multitude of types of smokers. There are the professional pipe smokers who quietly puff away and don't inhale. Then, there are the pipe smokers who puff away and inhale cummulus clouds of smoke during most of their waking moments. The same with cigar smokers; there are the puffers-only and the *suction pumps*, whose insides most likely resemble the interior of a blast furnace!

And, then, we have the cigarette smoker. There are some who actually smoke cigarettes (many of them) and never inhale. My father was in this category. Then, there are the fortunate few who smoke only when they go out of town on business, or only when they attend a party where there is social drinking, or only at night or only on high holidays, which ever comes first. Then, of course, we have everybody's favorite, the *chain* cigarette smoker.

Most of us remember how we got started smoking. Many of us sneaked a cigarette from a parent's pack and lit up at a tender age—11 or so seems to be the average age. We coughed a few times and wondered how the hell Dad and/or Mom could smoke the stuff. But, somehow, we persisted. I wasn't above picking up butts from the street and going off somewhere with buddies to have a clandestine smoking experience. I actually took the tobacco from butts and filled my *bubble pipe!* I even took lead pencil shavings and wrapped them in a sheet of small pad paper and puffed away on what must have been a truly lethal concoction. But what the hell did I know? I was a kid!

My generation, by the way, sneaked around and fanned the air in the bathroom in a *panic* when we thought our parents would catch us in the act. But today's pubescent crowd apparently has come out of the closet in a big (and frightening!) way. Even if you're a heavy smoker over age 20, there is no way you can witness the large groups of JUNIOR high school students (girls, as well as boys), inhaling away like real pros, without experiencing a surge of genuine sadness. All of which reminds us: How many of you smoke like chimneys and urge your children *never* to take up the habit?

Now, let's take a look at some of the smokers we have known. You'll probably find yourself here someplace.

● REASONABLE: (There really isn't any *reason*.) At the turn of the century, Joseph Grew was the U.S. Ambassador to Japan. His motto was "prohibition in nothing; temperance in all things." Grew, undoubtedly,

NO BUTTS ABOUT IT

knew *something*. There are many smokers who have the ability to enjoy smoking cigarettes, with a full inhale of each puff, without ever overdoing it. They have about five to 10 a day and go about their merry way. They can consider themselves to be truly blessed. I always figured Henry Fonda was in this category.

● WEIRDOS: As we mentioned earlier, there are some people who smoke *only* at parties, chain smoking all the while, and never touch another cigarette until the next social outing. I *do* actually know a man who smokes *only* when he leaves town on business. If he's away for a day or a week—or longer—he inhales with the best of them during the entire time. When his plane lands upon his arrival home, he reverts to being a non-smoker—even at parties.

● DIEHARDS: I know another fellow who was told by his doctor that he must *never* smoke another cigarette. He told his physician that he'd go along with him, on one condition. "What's that?" his doctor asked. "I insist on having one cigarette first thing in the morning." The doctor naturally asked "Why?" The patient said, "I need a cigarette in the morning so I can move my bowels." Since then, my acquaintance has had 365 cigarettes per *year*, except for leap year when he increases his intake by one.

● HOOKED: This category includes persons who inhale close to a pack a day—or more. They can't remember just how they got there. All they know is that they *need* to inhale cigarette smoke on a regular basis. If they don't, they find that they grow tense and irritable and are almost totally unable to do any meaningful work.

● HELPLESS: These poor souls smoke at least three packs a day and look it! As you'll see later in the book, many of these people reach the very top of their chosen field.

Whichever category you place yourself in, you are coming under increasing pressure to lay off the smoking habit. The Surgeons General scare the wits out of smokers every few weeks. More people are paying increasing attention to their quality of life. They happen to be non-smokers. They have lobbied for and have got airlines, many restaurants and others to segregate them from smokers. They have become increasingly vociferous in their complaints about smokers who violate their "space." I've witnessed near-fistfights on commuter trains when a non-smoker has spotted a guy in the non-smoking car, attempting to sneak a few puffs before he arrived at his station. "Hey, fella, this is a non-smoking car. If you want to smoke, get the hell out of here!" Just imagine how that hapless smoker felt. And, yet, a buck will get you a tenspot, that he's still smoking away and still trying to violate non-smokers's space if he has half a chance of getting away with it. He simply can't help it! It's sad—and sick. I know. I've been there.

In short, it is becoming much less acceptable in our society to smoke—period! More and more people are insisting that guests in their homes go outside if they must have a cigarette. (Remember when Hollywood columnists used to write cute stories about Doris Day—a Christian Scientist—having a no-smoking rule in her house? She

NO BUTTS ABOUT IT

was the exception; now she's becoming the rule.)

Violating the space of others is one thing (and it's very understandable that non-smokers give smokers holy hell about it), but try having a heart attack or some other disease linked to smoking and you enter a very special purgatory. Try, as I have, lighting up upon returning from a coronary-induced hospital stay when you can't fight the urge any longer. The spouse and close friends don't hesitate these days to ream you up one side and down the other. Just as you take the pack out, they look right at you and say things like: "Don't do that, please don't light that." Or . . . "You've got to be out of your mind! You're going to kill yourself; you know that, don't you?!"

It's not easy anymore, that's for sure!
I was having lunch with a group once, lighting up constantly during cocktails and between courses. A lady leaned across the table and looked me right in the eye and said, "How long have you been smoking?" It was a direct question so I gave a direct answer: "Most of my life." She asked how much I smoked. "Constantly," I chuckled in reply. "That's rather stupid, isn't it?" she said, and went back to her Chinese food. Her comment shocked the hell out of me. Suddenly, I felt guilty as hell. I felt even guiltier later on when I learned from another at the table that the lady had recently lost her daughter, you guessed it, to cancer!

But, what most light smokers or non-smokers don't understand about chain smokers is that chain smoking is an integral part of one's life. The chain smoker *always* has a raw throat and *always* has a terrible taste in the mouth.

NO BUTTS ABOUT IT

But heavy smoking keeps the motor running. It's as simple as that. Feeling like shit most of the time is part of the game.

For the chain smoker, life is cyclical. Unlike the nonsmoker or very light smoker (who, upon arising, will feel as well as they're going to feel that day), the chain smoker actually thrives on the ups and downs that accompany the constant inhalation of smoke. The heavy smoker starts slowly and perks up in stages throughout the day. By the time he or she goes to bed, the downturn has begun and total exhaustion has probably set in by the time the lights go out. (There *are* a number of very well known heavy smokers who *never* seem to slow down. But, somehow, they've been given special genes or something like that, that sets them apart from the norm. They're weird.)

To call smoking a "nasty habit" could very well be one of history's colossal understatements. Ponder this: by noon the chain smoker has gone through at least a pack. He or she has a couple of cocktails with lunch, which spurs increasingly rapid smoking. The alcohol works on the system throughout the afternoon, calling for a stepped-up rate of smoke inhalation. (The motor is not only running; it's revving up to Mach 1!)

The ride home from work simply means more smoking. A couple of drinks before dinner just keeps that motor clicking away at fever pitch. After a few hours sleep, the chain smoker gets out of bed and—first thing—lights up to greet the new day, through a glass, *very* darkly.

Heavy smokers remain in a nicotine-saturated state indefinitely, until, if they are lucky, they "sleep in" on a

NO BUTTS ABOUT IT

weekend, long enough to give the motor a slight rest. Their motor slows to a more reasonable RPM, but only until the cycle begins anew, at a party or at the office or *anyplace* where constant smoking occurs.

Whatever the level of smoking, whether it is simply habit with no inhalation or the addictive chain variety, once the smoker has sense enough to stop, he or she finds out that, horror of horrors, stopping is not only difficult—it is impossible! I have actually stopped smoking for a few days (proud as a peacock), only to pick up a pack of cigarettes, regrettably left lying about, and lighted up and found myself back to smoking WITHOUT EVEN KNOWING WHAT I WAS DOING! Now, that's certainly a habit that is hard to break. Agreed?

Surveys have proved that well over 50 million Americans smoke and that *most* of them want to stop. You know why most of those frustrated millions want to stop and you know why most of them don't stop. They can't stop and you know all of the reasons why this is so. Right?

THINKING TIME!

Use this space to write down, as best you can, your first experience with smoking. Also try to describe various times when you have felt your worst physically, as a result of smoking.

WHAT TYPE ARE YOU?

    Reasonable _____

    Weirdo _____

    Diehard _____

    Hooked _____

    Helpless _____

DO YOU HAVE TEENAGE CHILDREN?

    Yes _____

    No _____

DO YOU LET THEM SMOKE?

    Yes _____

    No _____

HOW MUCH MONEY DO YOU SPEND ON SMOKING EACH YEAR?

"Nasty Cough You've Got There"

DON'T GET OLDER, GET BETTER!

Any smoker worth his salt has gone through a pack of cigarettes by noon. A few heavy smokers make it a rule not to have their first cigarette until after bathing and dressing for the day and having something to eat. *Then,* they begin. The really dedicated smoker probably has the first cigarette under way by the time his or her feet hit the floor in the morning. They have a cigarette on the john, while shaving, while dressing. On average, this major-league smoker has had at least four or five cigarettes *before* that first cup of coffee.

Heavy smokers *must* have cigarettes available in the same room — preferably *on* them. Otherwise, they begin to grow tense. These are the persons who won't go to the bathroom without a pack in their hands or answer a telephone or go into a meeting or a social gathering without their security sticks at the ready. They simply cannot do it!

But if they've ever tried to stop smoking (and, remember, most of them have — many times), they *know* they will feel much better when off the weed than when on. Any smoker with access to a newspaper or other periodicals knows that smoking constricts the blood vessels. Some years ago, *The Reader's Digest* made the obvious point that, because of this constricting action, sex, by definition, is less enjoyable among smokers than it is among non-smokers. The nerve ends simply cannot react to their fullest when encumbered by constriction. Therefore, the bells ring louder and the birds fly overhead faster for the sexually involved *non-smoker*. Makes sense, doesn't it?

Now *there* is a very attractive incentive to stop smoking immediately. Can you imagine?! We are told that by not smoking, we will enjoy sex more. This isn't one of those esoteric inducements like better overall health or whiter teeth or non-yellowed fingers. We are actually told (by *The Reader's Digest*, no less) that we will enjoy one of life's greatest pleasures *more* if we don't smoke. But, no, the heavy smoker keeps puffing away and copulating away, indifferent to what he or she is missing. Let's put it this way: If you don't care about having better sex, what in the hell *do* you care about?

For those who have stopped and started, time after time, during their smoking careers, probably the biggest reason why they are constantly thinking of stopping again (besides the obvious fear of cancer or heart disease) is that

NO BUTTS ABOUT IT

they are fully aware that when they are not smoking, they feel better. It takes about two full days off the weed to discover that when awakening in the morning, the body seems to wake up about the same time as the eyes. Unlike the smoker who historically has kidded about "getting the heart started" each morning.

The heavy smoker wakes up each morning with a feeling akin to having had someone jump on his or her chest all night. It is slow going every morning for the smoker. No wonder. Notwithstanding an outwardly healthy appearance, packs of cigarettes each day (and all that constriction) must make a mess out of one's innards. All circulation is adversely affected by the smoking habit. The smoker knows this. What follows is what a smoker feels each day and what a smoker who has kicked the habit feels by comparison. First, our beloved smokers:

SMOKERS

- Wake up with a groggy feeling after eight hours sleep. Have trouble breathing properly. Experience a taste in the mouth not unlike old sweat socks.
- Walk stiff-legged to bathroom, possibly with a cigarette.
- Take a shower and cough frequently and spit mightily to clear the throat of the previous day's smoking activity.
- Drive to work (or to the station) with the vague thought that a lighted cigarette has been left in a very dangerous place, endangering home and family members. Thought passes.

- Fill ashtray at work (or litter out-of-doors) frequently throughout the day. Can't answer a telephone or hammer a nail without lighting up first. Stop smoking while eating food at lunch, but make up for this by having a couple of "quick ones," along with the tooth picking.
- Arrive home physically beat. Smoke throughout evening in a very sedentary position while watching television for hours.
- Just barely able to don night clothes, reluctantly snuff out last butt of the day before turning off light. Really need a good night's sleep.
- If they wake up during the night, a cigarette *always* keeps them company.

REFORMED SMOKERS
(Two days off weed)

- Wake up and notice that they actually *feel* awake. They are far less listless than they were two days before.
- Notice that they seem to talk to their mate more than they did before. They are aware of more things around them.
- Conclude that they feel stronger throughout the day — and have sense of personal pride that they are doing something (finally) that is extremely positive.
- During lunch, notice that their food tastes better than before. In fact, they get the feeling that they are actually tasting food for the first time in an age.
- Arrive home feeling relatively fit and, instead of plopping down in front of the TV, find themselves looking for things to do around the house.

NO BUTTS ABOUT IT

- Make love that night. GANGBUSTERS!!

The above examples are but a few distinctions heavy smokers know exist while they're smokers and while they are non-smokers. Persons who have never smoked, don't know what they are missing. (But there we go again, trying to find humor in this truly deadly subject.)

Bet you can relate to this one:

True story of two brothers. (You've probably had much the same conversation yourself.)

FIRST BROTHER: "How long has it been since you stopped smoking?"

SECOND BROTHER: "I guess it's been six or seven years now."

FIRST BROTHER: "I don't know how in the hell you do it. I stopped once for six months and started up again. I can't even remember why I started."

SECOND BROTHER: "I feel a lot better. I can do yard work all day now. Before, I had to stop every fifteen minutes, because I kept getting tired."

FIRST BROTHER: "I know. Every time I stop smoking, I've got so much more energy."

SECOND BROTHER: "I don't even think about smoking anymore."

FIRST BROTHER: "Every time I've ever stopped, I've *thought* of smoking the whole time I was off."

SECOND BROTHER: "Why don't you just stop?"

FIRST BROTHER: "I will. I feel so much better when I do. I will, soon."

(Wanna bet!)

NO BUTTS ABOUT IT

THINKING TIME!

Take a few minutes to jot down an experience or two that describes how you feel in the morning. If you've ever stopped, compare the "before and after" feelings.

_____

_____

_____

_____

_____

_____

DO YOU KNOW PEOPLE WHO HAVE STOPPED?
(Write down their names.)

_____

_____

_____

_____

_____

"Do you smoke after intercourse?"
"I don't know. I've never looked."

NO BUTTS ABOUT IT

TAIN'T FUNNY, MCGEE

"He laughed in the face of death," is a phrase that has been used to describe heroism through the years. But it is said that heroes die but once and that cowards die many deaths — playing *nicotine roulette*!

Laughing in the face of death (or ugly, crippling disease) is what we know more than 50 million Americans do every day of their lives. But they're not heroes. Not by a long shot. Most of them would admit, as we've all heard and said ourselves: "I'm crazy to do it, I know that, but I can't stop." We can't stop, even though we know it's more harmful than overeating or most other forms of over-indulgence. So . . . we laugh it off.

We laugh off what can only be described as an idiotic habit. We don't like to think of ourselves as idiots, so we try not to think about how downright foolish we are to

24
NO BUTTS ABOUT IT

smoke and are not above making jokes about the subject.

Probably no publication has attempted to take the fun out of smoking more so than *The Reader's Digest.* For many years, *The Digest* has carried factual articles describing the ills of smoking. The magazine has pulled no punches. Its articles search out the goriest details that are blatantly aimed at scaring its millions of smoking readers into dropping the habit.

An article in 1968 has become famous because it did scare the hell out of a lot of people, including me. It was so scary that it undoubtedly prompted many readers to stop smoking forever or to stop for as long as they could, before the details of the article subsided from their consciousness and they resumed their suicidal ways. The star of the article was a man who had just undergone an operation for throat cancer and, as a result, would spend the rest of his life without a voice box. In short, he lost his ability to speak normally — forever. He had just become one of those people who have holes surgically installed in their throats so that they can continue to communicate via gulping air and forming understandable words in slow, laborious cadences. The scene took place in the recovery ward of the cancer section of the hospital. The article described this unfortunate man, a very heavy smoker who apparently had paid the price by losing his ability to ever use his own voice again. He was sitting in the ward, not long after his operation, *smoking!* He had actually rigged up a device to which he attached his omnipresent cigarette and was smoking away, through his *throat!*

This was, obviously, an extreme case of nicotine

addiction, of a habit too difficult to break. But, anyone reading this, who *knows* he or she smokes too much and who has known the panic that sets in when a supply of cigarettes is not available, would agree that that intrepid cancer patient, though exceptional, is not beyond believability.

What makes it truly difficult to relate to that cancer victim (and other stories we hear about) is that we very seldom have first-hand experience with such cases. We hear about them or read about them. That's about as far as it goes. But, frequently, even having first-hand knowledge of what heavy smoking can do, does not deter the hooked smoker from continuing to puff away.

For instance: The following story is true and is one that some of you reading this book have probably experienced yourselves.

During my heyday as a heavy smoker, I heard that a former colleague had had "that" operation. Another case of a man in his mid-thirties with a fine family, home, and job who, never again, would speak normally. I hadn't seen him for a few years, but the fact that I once knew him well, brought the message home with infinitely more impact than any mere magazine article could ever do. He was my age. I could relate to him and his misfortune. The familiar tremors of fear crept into my psyche when I heard about him. I made a mental note that, soon, I should seriously go about stopping smoking, myself.

About six months later, I attended a business function, at which I went through the normal business of eating tons of *hors d'oeuvre*, drinking far too many cocktails and

NO BUTTS ABOUT IT

smoking one cigarette after another. What made that evening different from all the rest was that my former colleague was there. When I heard that he was there (he still had his sales job and, I was told, had learned to speak by gulping air faster than anyone could have hoped), I sought him out. He was a good man and I wanted to see him and talk with him and let him know that I wished him well. I *didn't* tell him that I was scared to death about what my reaction would be when I saw him.

He looked exactly the same as when I last saw him. He was having a drink. He greeted me as normally as anyone could have. I told him how great he looked. We carried on a perfectly normal conversation. I even found myself thinking it was very natural for him to be speaking in gulps and through his throat. He did look great and behaved normally. I wanted to cry. Moreover, I wanted never to have another cigarette as long as I lived. But I continued to smoke heavily for many years after that jarring experience. The point is, even seeing it *first hand* didn't make me stop. I wanted to. I simply couldn't. Not yet.

Some years back, comedian Shelley Berman (whatever happened to him?) had a best selling album on which he had a routine about various plights of smokers. It was (still is!) funny as hell. During the routine, Berman described the hapless smoker who puts his fingers on his cigarette, intent on taking it from his mouth after a good drag. All dedicated smokers laughed heartily as Berman painted a verbal portrait of the man's fingers slipping down the length of the cigarette — which had decided on its own to stay stuck to the lips — only to have them glide over the

NO BUTTS ABOUT IT

burning end, suffering acute pain in the process. Berman had expertly described an experience with which all cigarette smokers are only too familiar.

A second routine had Berman parked in his car at a red light. The same thing happened, only (as we all know) the sparks descended into his crotch and Berman described the resultant panic, as he feverishly tried to remove the sparks from the vulnerable area with his hand. Having done so successfully, he looked out the car window only to conclude that the passengers in the bus next to him thought the worst about Berman's apparent sexual abberration.

Phil Harris used to sing a song that said something about smoking cigarettes . . . till you smoke yourself to death. That song has been around for many years and it is frighteningly true. The only problem is that it doesn't stop many of us from inviting illness or death, which is what we do when we continue to smoke cigarettes. Stories of John Wayne losing a lung or Jerry Lewis having a double bypass or anything *The Reader's Digest* wants to throw at us don't stop us. It is nothing short of incredible how addictive we can be in the face of such weighty, truly *frightening* evidence.

Ponder this: We put rubbers on to keep our feet dry when it's raining, because we don't want to ruin our shoes or catch a cold. We pop vitamin pills to help keep us healthy. We do various exercises to do the same. We use suntan lotion to prevent severe sunburn. We use goggles when we perform do-it-yourself chores around the house, because we don't want to lose an eye. We usually try to get a reasonable amount of sleep so our bodies will not

NO BUTTS ABOUT IT

become overly tired. We do all of these things and much, much more to maintain a modicum of healthiness. But, we continue to smoke cigarette after cigarette, even though we are told that, among other things, we can possibly lose our voice or a lung to the ravages of cigarette tars or, if that doesn't happen, we can suffer from heart disease because of the nicotine. We can be disabled or die, but we continue to smoke. As Shakespeare might advise . . . "must give us pause."

When the U.S. Surgeon General got into the act during 1964, there was a funny line that made the rounds: "Since I heard about cigarettes causing cancer, I've doubled up on my smoking just to see if there's anything to it."

You can literally die from laughing at that one. It is nothing short of amazing how ironclad our resolve can be when it comes to consciously doing something that can do us grave harm. The cowboy rides serenely into the sunset, smoking away on his high selling brand. He doesn't know it, but he could very well be heading for his last roundup.

Smoking is considered so dangerous by health authorities that advertising cigarettes on television has long been *banned*! What a slap on the wrists that prohibition has been. A skull and cross bones on a bottle of iodine keeps us from taking a swig of the stuff. But a printed warning on cigarette packs that says: "Warning: The Surgeon General Has Determined That Cigarette Smoking Is Dangerous To Your Health" doesn't mean a damned thing to most of us. Maybe Johnny still can't read, but we can,
can't we?

NO BUTTS ABOUT IT

THINKING TIME!

Make note below of some funny one liners *you've* heard about smoking. Include descriptions of times when you were actually frightened by hearing or reading of a smoking-induced tragedy.

_____

_____

_____

_____

_____

_____

_____

_____

_____

HAVE YOU EVER BURNED YOUR CLOTHES, SELF, FURNITURE?

    Yes _____

    No _____

Stop-Start-Stop-St

NO BUTTS ABOUT IT

TREADMILLS ARE HABIT FORMING

We've made general remarks about the stop-start syndrome. Let's get specific:

I remember as if it were 10 minutes ago when I sat in our living room one afternoon and lighted a cigarette in front of my parents. I was 17 at the time. I had been an unofficial smoker for about three years. One day I simply bit the bullet and struck a match for independence across the room from my mother and father.

My mother never smoked. My father smoked cigars, cigarettes and a pipe. He also chewed tobacco, usually *Beechnut*, in a bag, but he preferred to work on a *plug* of tobacco. A plug of tobacco is one of the vilest tasting things in the world. Dad loved them. I actually enjoyed chewing (at age seven!) a *chaw* of *Beechnut*, which was rather sweet. But I gagged whenever I attempted to work on a small chunk of the rock-hard plug Dad managed to carry around in his sweater pocket for what seemed to be *years*! The man who introduced me to the joys of chewing *Beechnut* was a farmer. He smoked a pipe and chewed tobacco — at the same time.

I didn't even think of stopping smoking until my college years. I managed to become a member of the lacrosse team and had a coach who had the crazy idea that to get fit enough to run up and down a 120-yard field, one had to EXERCISE! Having gained a modicum of fitness, I'd consider becoming a non-smoker — now and then. I didn't really have to quit smoking because I was a goalie, a second-string goalie. It is a truism that second-string lacrosse goalies don't play much during regular games. In fact, they don't play at all. What I did was serve as a battering ram during practice sessions during the week *before* the game on Saturday.

Anyhow, when I decided to give myself a chance to become the first-string goalie when the spot became open because of graduation, I stopped smoking cold turkey at the midnight that ushered in January, 1954. I got myself as fit as I've ever been in my life, made the first team and missed smoking cigarettes desperately.

Now get this: I stopped smoking on January 1. Our final game was in mid-May. As soon as I showered and dressed and arrived at the restaurant for a team celebration, I DID IT! I raced to the cigarette machine and obtained a pack of cigarettes. I was a smoker again. I began the process that leads from total fitness to an outward appearance of fitness and an inner feeling of

NO BUTTS ABOUT IT

chagrin, self-loathing and, really, rather filthy innards. (I've always assumed.)

This trend continued for about 25 years. With relentless regularity I resolved not to smoke. I would crumple up an almost full pack of cigarettes, toss it into the trash can and *minutes* later, I would retrieve said crumpled package and try to find an unbroken cigarette. If I found one, I'd straighten it out and light up. If all cigarettes were broken, I'd light up the longest portion I could find. I could always forecast how serious I was about never smoking another cigarette as long as I lived by the severity with which I crushed the package. If I knew in my heart that this was just another practice run, I wouldn't squeeze the package hard enough to actually break the cigarettes.

What makes stopping so difficult (and I do mean stopping one day at a time because stopping forever is impossible, as the saying is) is that it is so easy to blame others or some *thing* for making you start again. Run these through your "I've been there" machine:

• Resolve to give up smoking, extinguishing the *last ever* cigarette before going to sleep. Wake up and take strong exception to your wife saying something hairbrained like, "Good morning, sweetheart." I mean, it is one of life's wonders how quickly a decision to stop smoking turns us into the epitome of Mr. Hyde. In fact, I've had some of my best arguments immediately after deciding to stop smoking. The kicker *always* is: You get so mad you start smoking again — on the spot! And, at least I did, you usually blame your resumption of the habit on the *argument*.

- Stop smoking and go to a party where *everyone* else is smoking. It's a *gimme*, really. We tell ourselves that if we only had not gone to the party we would have stayed off. It's always convenient to blame the situation.

- Stop smoking for a fair amount of time and, one day, spot a pack of cigarettes on the coffee table or, let's face it, *anywhere*. We glance about to see if our conscience is watching and, sure enough, are back among the *World Class Smokers!* If only our wife (son, daughter, father, mother — check one) hadn't left that pack right out there where we could see it, we never would have started again. This rationale helps us over the rough spots connected with failure.

We always find excuses, far from our own doorstep, for behavior which is *our* responsibility. We can (and do) find scapegoats galore. We actually tell ourselves that if we were just left alone, we would be able to stop. It's not us, we conclude; it's, well, it's the rest of the world that's to blame for what we do.

The times they are changing, as the saying is. It's difficult to go through a day without seeing a plethora of warnings about smoking cigarettes or drinking alcohol. Isolate yourself from broadcast or print media and a bumper sticker or billboard will get you if you don't watch out. The pressure's on, no doubt about it.

We're into fitness. Just about everybody is wearing running shoes and warm-up suits. Show up in this attire and people will smile and say something like, "Hey, you're really going for it, huh?"

Start smoking after trying to give it up and friends say, "Taking dumb pills, again, huh?"

"Don't you ever inhale?"
Said to Peter Lorre

NO BUTTS ABOUT IT

THE SMOKER'S HALL OF FAME

If only a bunch of obvious *dumb-dumbs* smoked heavily, it would seem to be infinitely easier for those who consider themselves to be reasonably intelligent to stop once they started. *Everyone* knows that non-smokers are better off than heavy smokers. But it is difficult to convince someone that a pack or more a day can do great harm when he or she can point out far too many examples of heavy smokers who have made it or are making it in this world of ours in a *very* big way.

Sure, for example, we can tell our kids that smoking has no place in athletics. But what in the hell do we tell them when they can look around them and come up with myriad examples of heavy smokers who are at the very top in sports and other fields? Many who made it big were very heavy smokers during most of their adult life, but did stop smoking. But, the determined smoker might say, they did much of their best work while inhaling packs a day. Many people, in fact, tell themselves that they will stop — after they've enjoyed the habit for enough years to get their fair share. "It worked for others, why not me?", they tell themselves. That's what I told myself.

History is fraught with top people who, obviously, were, or still are, addicted to the weed. What follows is a very small list of obvious inductees into the *Smokers Hall of Fame*:

ENTERTAINMENT

Humphrey Bogart: Bogart was probably the most dedicated smoker in film history. What the heck — in history — period. He had his own special way of holding a cigarette in his hands, of putting it into his lips. He *always* had a burning cigarette. Still photographs of him working on his beloved sailboat show him, cigarette firmly between lips and eyes obviously being seared, steering or handling lines without missing a puff. Bogart had a serious cough for many years and his death by cancer probably was at least, in part, a result of those years of heavy, heavy smoking.

Sammy Davis: Sammy Davis once announced that, because of a promise to Frank Sinatra, he would no longer hold a cigarette in his hands while performing. This had to be quite a compromise because Davis, for years, entertained the world as few men ever have, enveloped by a haze of cigarette smoke.

Richard Burton: This man had to have had one of the few God-given voices ever bestowed upon a human

NO BUTTS ABOUT IT

being. And yet, Burton — in the face of all the evidence — smoked constantly and inhaled more deeply than people who don't depend on their voice for their livelihood. It started to show on him a long time before he passed away.

Spencer Tracy: Tracy was apparently the *sneakiest* smoker of them all. A friend mentioned once that Tracy didn't smoke. Tracy allowed as how that, yes, he certainly did smoke — heavily. The star explained that he was an insomniac and that when he retired to bed, he read most of the night, with a pot of coffee on the boil and smoked cigarettes non-stop. He simply didn't smoke when he got out of bed in the morning.

Dean Martin: Is there *anyone* who ever saw Dean Martin without a cigarette? He almost chews them! It is not without good reason that Martin frequently clears his throat during his appearances on the tube. Unlike Bogart's style of *cupping* the cigarette in his hand, Martin chooses to use the *spread eagle* technique. That is, his fingers are spread widely and the omnipresent cigarette is tucked securely between the index and middle fingers.

Robert Donat: This fine actor (his *Mr. Chips* beat out Clark Gable's *Rhett Butler* for an Oscar) went through Alfred Hitchcock's *The 39 Steps* hardly ever being without a cigarette. He was handcuffed to Madeleine Carroll throughout much of the film, jumped from a train and ate a sandwich through omnipresent billows of cigarette smoke. Truly World Class.

Jerry Lewis: This comedian raised many millions of dollars during his annual telethons for muscular dystrophy and managed to go through seemingly millions of deeply inhaled cigarettes during each marathon fund raiser. This was irony at its most awesome, until Lewis walked into a Las Vegas hospital and walked out sometime after a double by-pass operation.

Bob Fosse: Open heart surgery did not deter this famous choreographer ("All That Jazz," "Dancin'," "Pippin") from continuing a multi-pack habit. It was reported that concerned friends had actually formed a special group whose purpose it was to convince him to stop!

Peter Lawford: A member of the Bogart-Sinatra-Davis "Rat Pack" a few years ago, Lawford obviously decided it was better to join 'em rather than fight 'em. Lawford, like Bogart and Martin, was *never* seen without a cigarette.

Erroll Flynn: It is virtually impossible to see a still photograph of Flynn without a cigarette in mouth or hand. Even while receiving a trophy for having just won a tennis match! Flynn also hit booze and drugs pretty good, but does anyone not believe that constant smoking had *something* to do with his passing away before his fiftieth birthday?

Tyrone Power: Not only was Power reportedly bisexual and a one-time lover of Flynn, he had almost the same smoking habits. Following a Marine Corps (Reserves) examination that termed him fit as a fiddle, Power dropped dead while filming a movie at about 45 years of age. Any questions?

Tallulah Bankhead: She smoked so much that she always looked as if she had a cloud following her around. She was another heavy drinker for whom nicotine and alcohol formed the all-too-familiar, *necessary* combination during every waking moment.

Peter Lorre: This truly great actor smoked so much that, near the end, he could barely breathe. Someone once asked him, while trying to see Lorre through the clouds of smoke he developed around him: "Peter, don't you ever inhale?"

Bette Davis: Like Bogart, she and the cigarette became synonymous. The big difference, however, is that Miss Davis explained that she never inhaled. Maybe that's why she's still around and Bogart isn't.

Edward R. Murrow: This great newscaster is included in this category because of his television program "Person to Person." He and Bogart must be fighting for the top spot in the smoking pantheon, because Murrow was truly one of the all-time greats. It has been said that, like Tracy, he smoked a pack of cigarettes from the time he went to bed until he got up. While testifying before the Senate Foreign Relations Committee, prior to becoming head of the U.S. Information Service, Murrow did not smoke. Midway through the testimony, one Senator, a fan, asked Murrow why he had not smoked during the time at the table. "I didn't think it was permitted," Murrow replied. As soon as the Senator explained that there was nothing against witnesses smoking, Murrow lighted up.

Robert Blake: This fine actor (*In Cold Blood, Baretta*) is a shining example of how difficult it is to give up the smoking habit. Blake frequently appears on the *Johnny Carson Show* and other "talk" formats and regales the audience with tales of the "turkeys" he has to deal with in filmdom. For some time, Blake appeared on these shows holding an unlighted cigarette. He's off the weed, but *needed* to hold one in his hand to *stay* off! This is the ultimate "crutch" of a heavy smoker who has stopped, but hasn't yet really *quit*!

Nat King Cole: This all-time singing favorite was a very heavy smoker. One day, he received the news all heavy smokers fear: he had cancer — terminal cancer. Cole reportedly sent for a close friend. When the friend arrived, Cole asked him simply, "Why me?" A very understandable question, one we all would probably ask. I heard a sermon once that suggested a very reasonable reply to Cole's question: "Why not?"

Johnny Carson: For all these many years, Carson has been puffing away on his "Tonight" show, although he's cut down somewhat on camera. The interesting thing about Carson is that, besides having what seems to be a healthy smoking habit, he is reportedly dedicated to physical fitness. So far, he hasn't caught on to an obvious reason why he should stop and *really* opt for physical fitness. He simply has to look closely at his partner during all these years and notice that Ed McMahon seems to be having the time of his life — *without* smoking.

Oscar Levant: One of the truly great wits and a brilliant pianist, Levant had a gargantuan smoking habit. It is doubtful that his lungs were *ever* relieved of clouds of smoke as he puffed and puffed and puffed and inhaled and inhaled and inhaled. Jack Paar had Levant on his show shortly before Levant died. He was, literally, a shadow of his former self. Truly sad and shocking!

NO BUTTS ABOUT IT

Jackie Gleason: It baffles me that the American Medical Association hasn't contracted with a "hit man" to deal with this very funny guy. From what we've seen and heard, Gleason doesn't spend a waking moment without a cigarette *and* drink in hand and his girth indicates that he is on a first name basis with calories. Like Dean Martin, Gleason favors the "spread eagle" mode of holding his cigarette. If he weren't an avid golfer, I'd swear it's because he can't bend his fingers! Gleason was born with a set of *those* genes that enable some of us to violate all health rules and still remain active well into the twilight years.

Redd Foxx: It's obvious that the NAACP got together years ago and voted to have one of its own give Gleason a run for his money. "Go forth, Redd," they must have said, "and show them honkies how to *really* smoke!" Foxx was a guest once on Tom Snyder's ill-fated *Tomorrow* show. Not once was he without a burning cigarette. I got the feeling that Snyder sat there in envy (not to mention awe) of his smoke enshrouded guest.

Noel Coward: When seen just before his death, this creative genius could just barely move — and he could just barely speak because of what the omnipresent cigarette and almost non-stop inhaling had done to him. An intelligent man who obviously concluded years before: "What the hell?"

David Janssen: This giant of television had a persona that made it appear that he had just enough energy to lift his head. He *always* looked tired. Heavy drinking reportedly helped, but a constant inhalation of cigarettes certainly didn't pep him up. His sudden death before he reached age 50 should not be a surprise to anyone.

GOVERNMENT

Lyndon Johnson: A very heavy smoker most of his adult life, Johnson had a heart attack while he was Majority Leader of the U.S. Senate. On the way to the hospital in an ambulance, Johnson took out a pack of cigarettes. The attending physician admonished him not to light up. Johnson reportedly said: "Doc, just let me have one more and I'll never smoke another one." He did have one more and went on to become President.

Jody Powell: Press Secretary to born-again, non-smoking Jimmy Carter, Powell was another very heavy smoker — and it showed. Powell is extremely intelligent (nearly a Ph.D), but obviously couldn't make it through a White House day without constant inhaling. Most photographs of him during Carter's term of office were a dead giveaway that he was on a first name basis with nicotine.

Everett Dirksen: The late Republican Senate bigwig had one of the most recognizable voices in this country and was a famous orator. Near the end, his words just made it out of his mouth as he was trying to get enough breath to continue speaking. Obviously sick and suffering discomfort, Dirksen still managed to puff away ceaselessly. His inhale was so deep, the smoke must have reached his toes!

Dwight Eisenhower: Ike made it through all the stress of World War II on a mega-pack habit. He reportedly stopped soon after the war when he noticed that he had lit a cigarette only to discover that he hadn't finished the first one. He concluded that this was ridiculous and stopped on the spot. Fifteen years later following a crucial cabinet meeting, Ike told someone: "I wanted a cigarette so bad in there I could taste it." (Instant reminder: You don't have to stop smoking for the rest of your life. Just stop smoking one day at a time.)

Franklin Roosevelt: FDR used a cigarette holder so he lost valuable time placing a cigarette into it before lighting up. Congestive heart disease plagued his later years but he kept on puffin' — constantly.

Dean Rusk: Secretary of State under Kennedy and Johnson, Rusk *always* smoked, wherever he happened to be. Why do you think he kept licking his lips?

ATHLETICS

Fred Bilitnicoff: This former premier wide receiver for the *Oakland* (now Los Angeles) *Raiders* during their championship years admitted to a three-pack-a-day habit. But — and here's the rationale that enabled him to puff away *all* day — and still run his intricate pass patterns: He said he only inhaled *one* of the three packs. As baseball announcer, Mel Allen, would say: "How about *that!*"

Joe DiMaggio: The greatest baseball centerfielder in history (an official vote of experts makes him so) can be spotted frequently in still photographs smoking in the *Yankees's* locker room following a game during his heyday, or socially puffing away with a style that clearly indicated that smoking was natural and enjoyable to him. He said he and others even smoked *during* games, hidden

NO BUTTS ABOUT IT

away in the dugout. Imagine how much better he would have been if he hadn't smoked!

Whitey Ford: Ford was another Yankee great and one of the best clutch pitchers in baseball history. Following his active career, Ford picked up a few bucks doing testimonials for *Bantron* advertisements, claiming that *Bantron* (a nicotine substitute that's supposed to get you over the physiological hump when you stop) helped him kick the smoking habit.

Earl Weaver: When he was manager of the Baltimore Orioles, Weaver didn't have to be in good shape but, as the leader of one of the best teams in baseball, he became famous as a heavy smoker during the 1979 World Series. The television camera constantly panned in on him in a nervous state in the dugout (he had stopped — again!). The commentator made repeated references to Weaver's nickname for his ace reliever, whom Weaver called "Two-Pack." This was a reference to whenever the reliever was on the mound, Weaver went through two packs of cigarettes because of the added tension created by the erratic hurler.

Ben Hogan: When Hogan was the premier golfer on the professional circuit, fans used to say when he was starting his move toward another championship, "The Eagle is flying." The cigarette butts were flying, too, because Hogan and cigarettes kept *very* close company. When he wasn't driving a ball straight toward the pin, he was puffing away, drawing nicotine and tars and assorted gases straight toward his lungs.

Arnold Palmer: The same goes for Palmer. When Arnie was delighting his "Army" by hitching up his trousers and walking pell-mell toward the ball to strike it again in one of his famous come-from-behind victories, he was smoking and tossing away butts with abandon. Palmer became almost as famous for his many attempts to kick the smoking habit as he did for his peerless golf game.

Honorable Mention: During Bjorn Borg's magnificent defense of his Wimbledon title against John McEnroe in 1980, the TV cameras frequently panned in on his attractive fiancee who was nervously watching her husband-to-be from the "Friends's Box." Every time I saw her, she was either lighting up or inhaling to beat the band. Any smoker worth his or her nicotine knew that young lady was far more exhausted from watching the match (and chain smoking) than Borg was after *playing* five sets of gruelling tennis.

Most Honorable Mention: Any Japanese businessman.

HAIG NEVER HAD A CHANCE

Ever wonder why Alexander Haig had such a tough time of it as Secretary of State? I never did. It was quite obvious to me why there were persistent reports of personality clashes between him and other members of the Reagan Administration. Soon after Haig ascended to First Secretary, *Time Magazine* casually mentioned that Haig was *trying* to give up cigarettes! The article explained that Haig "sneaked" a cigarette now and then. Shortly before he left the Cabinet, *Time* ran a photo of Haig at the United Nations. Earphones in place, he was publicly taking a big inhale. When I saw that, I knew it was just a matter of time. Lesson: if you're ever appointed to be Secretary of State, don't try to give up cigarettes at the same time.

NO BUTTS ABOUT IT

THINKING TIME!

Write down the names of celebrities *you* can think of who are heavy smokers.

48
NO BUTTS ABOUT IT

Take Two Aspirin Every Four Hours

NO BUTTS ABOUT IT

CRUTCHES I HAVE KNOWN

The American Cancer Society, the Smoke-Enders organization and the surprisingly few books written to help people stop smoking, rely very heavily upon "aids." The aids are supposed to help the new non-smoker over the psychological and physiological humps. Most of them prescribe a period before the actual cessation, during which the candidate for a healthier tomorrow is told how he or she should prepare for the ordeal ahead.

If you've read or heard anything at all on the subject of smoking, you know that one of the reasons you smoke is that you want to have something to do with your hands. Nay, you *must* have something to do with your hands. Smoking fulfills this digital need — in spades! One book suggests that the person who has stopped smoking can take up a musical instrument, such as the harmonica. This makes sense, except that I can think of few persons who are ready to take the abuse that is certain to come their way should they take out the ol' mouth organ during a business meeting and say, "Pardon me guys, while I whip off a tune or two to stay off the weed. I'm having quite a digital and oral reaction — one of the worst."

Ronald Reagan has done jelly bean manufacturers a big favor. He receives a lot of publicity by having a container of the candy in the Oval Office and elsewhere to satisfy his digital and oral needs since he stopped smoking years ago. Reagan's lungs are undoubtedly in much better shape than they were during his smoking days, but, very possibly, his gums have got to go.

We know that, when we stop smoking, it is all we can do not to emit primal screams as our systems cry out for a dose of the nicotine we have suddenly deprived them of. We climb the wall, we argue with our spouses over nothing, all because of the *reaction* our bodies endure when we go off the weed. Very reasonably, those doing the advising about halting the smoking habit suggest that, when the craving raises its ugly head, instead of reaching for a cigarette, we should take a few deep breaths instead. Makes sense. But, all too often, we say to hell with the deep breaths and grab a smoke. Just like that, we are back among the ranks of the hooked smoker.

The experts split hairs and claim that smoking is not really an addiction, but an *habituation*. I tend to think that heavy cigarette smoking is both! There is withdrawal. (Boy, is there withdrawal!). Those of us who have stopped might not writhe in agony as drug addicts apparently do when cut off from their fix, but we sure as hell find it difficult to do anything productive during the first couple of days of being without. This is why many of the experts advise that we choose a weekend or vacation during which to stop. The theory goes that to stop during the mid-work week is to put ourselves under undue strain and thereby run the risk of lighting up as soon as the first pressure comes our way.

We also hear about the fear of gaining weight when we stop. Studies reportedly have proved that the *average* weight gain is modest, about three to five pounds. Certainly some persons tend to gain much more. The point is that we know it would be better to gain a few pounds and stand a chance of living longer and better, but we use the weight gain excuse to stay hooked.

Because most heavy smokers have stopped many times, it is the reluctance to put ourselves through the easily recognizable grief again that deters us from *finally* stopping for good. I know of one chap, an absolutely brilliant lawyer and solid amateur tennis and backgammon player who stopped years ago after a multi-pack habit and has stayed off. He simply explains: "I'll never smoke again, because never, ever, will I put myself through the pain of stopping again." He says that with utter fear in his eyes.

The advice I give you in the next chapter that explains *how* to want to stop smoking gives details about how you go about it. But, it would be folly on my part to ignore the *aids* or *crutches* that you *think* you might need to make it all the way. I don't recommend harmonica playing or feasting on jelly beans, but what I do advise are proven ways to stay off cigarettes once you've declared to yourself (or to God or a spouse or *anybody!)* that you want to stop. Don't forget, *everybody* tells you that you must *want* to stop before you ever will. The final chapter of this book helps to remove the "Catch 22" of stopping, by adding a missing ingredient: that is, *how* to want to.

TIPS

● Whether you decide to gradually lead up to the big day by cutting down and prepping yourself mentally, or decide that "cold turkey" is the only way to fly, at least convince yourself that you actually *do* want to stop. Talk to yourself and pray if necessary, but build a good case for yourself with all the reasons you've always known why it is good for you to become a non-smoker. Look at a full ashtray and remind yourself of what a filthy habit it actually is. (Once again: if someone filled a balloon with smoke and asked you to inhale it, would you?) Pick out non-smokers you admire and decide that you are going to emulate them. START THE PROCESS!

● Go out and buy a supply of new soaps and after shave lotions, even a few new ties and shirts; a new dress, perfumes — you name it. This will help you get into the mood of becoming the *new* you. Decide that you are going to face the world as a non-smoker, as a better dressed and groomed and *conditioned* person. TRY TO LOOK BETTER!

● Physical fitness is vitally important to the person

NO BUTTS ABOUT IT

who is about to give up smoking. I have never experienced weight gain the many times I've stopped, because I have coupled a fitness program with the cessation. Exercise and limiting calories can work wonders in helping the new non-smoker to stay off the weed. Try to feel fit enough so that you won't want to lose that good feeling. Yes, do take a couple of deep breaths when that craving does occur. It helps. But also try to start walking or jogging just enough to give you that fit feeling. START THINKING FITNESS!

● This tip takes care of both the physiological and psychological problems when smoking has stopped: Whenever you feel the craving coming on, most likely the pulsation will attack your temples (they will pound) and hands (they will itch). Take those deep breaths and rub your temples briskly and rub your hands together — hard! Occasionally, go to the bathroom and give your face and hands a good massage with cold water and dry off by rubbing *hard*. You will find that you can rub your hands together briskly at a business meeting (where, naturally, you don't want to do anything embarrassing) and no one will be the wiser. RUB IT OUT!

● I don't recommend a harmonica, but I do recommend carrying a pencil or pen around with you, preferably ones with sharp edges to them. Simply rub the pencil or pen hard and you will find that this fills the digital need nicely. NO ONE WILL EVER KNOW!

● Shower (rubbing your body *very* briskly) and brush your teeth frequently during the first few days. This relieves tension that builds up and helps you maintain that "fit" feeling you have decided you want to keep forever.

WORK AT IT!

- One of the best crutches I've come across is arranging to have your teeth cleaned by your dentist's hygienist. Once you've got all of that plaque and stain off your pearly whites and see your real teeth for the first time in a long time, you will not want to do *anything* to dirty them again. This will be one of the best investments you will ever make — a modest one at that. **START WITH A CLEAN SLATE!**

- Periodically, slice a supply of carrots and celery. These "sticks" will replace the tobacco version you've been living with. They'll help keep you off cigarettes and will minimize any unwanted weight gain besides. The diet books keep coming off the presses, but we all know that there is only one effective diet: that is, you must burn off more calories than you consume each day. For men, I recommend keeping below 1,600 calories per day. Buy a calorie counter and you'll be surprised at how much you can eat of *anything* and still keep below 1,600 calories per day. For women, try keeping around 1,000 calories a day. **YOU CAN LOSE WEIGHT, TOO!**

- Try to keep mentally alert; keep concentrating. I have found that boredom has much to do with keeping smokers on the habit. People light up while waiting in line at the bank and elsewhere. We light up when we've finished a project and seem to have nothing to do for the moment. What else is there to do while watching hours of television? **STAY ALERT!**

- This is probably one of the most important tips I can give you. Keep reminding yourself what you think of

NO BUTTS ABOUT IT

yourself as a person. Do you want cancer of the throat? Do you want to have emphysema for the rest of your life? Because once you've got it, it's here to stay. Do you want to develop heart disease? Do you always want to be short of breath after moderate exercise? Do you want to set your bed (or people) on fire? Of course not. Once you stop, tell yourself repeatedly, **WHATEVER ELSE I AM, I AM NOT A SMOKER!**

THINKING TIME!

Write down some "crutches" you know have worked for you in the past. Write a short description of what you want the new you to look like.

_____

_____

_____

_____

_____

_____

_____

_____

_____

_____

_____

ASK YOURSELF THIS: IF THERE WERE NO TOBACCO, WHAT WOULD YOU SMOKE?

No time like the present!

SURPRISE!

Before you go on to the last chapter, I would like to take this time to inform you that you have *already* had your last cigarette. That's right. Here's why. As you've read through the book, you have probably been progressively making up your mind that, upon finishing the book you *will* light up one last cigarette and, then, go "cold turkey."

This is understandable because most of us, who decide to stop, do so with that "one last one" uppermost in mind as we gird our nerve ends for the ordeal ahead. Well, you can't have one last one. If you are still intent on doing just that, please stop reading! NOW. Close the book, have that cigarette and, then, reopen it to this page and start reading it from the beginning. Or, please, wait until you decide you're really serious about becoming an ex-smoker.

Please don't be dismayed or frightened by the suddenness of all this. If you can honestly say that you've already had your last one, what I have to say in the next chapter will make you glad that you agreed to follow my instructions. AND ... you will be surprised at how easy it all was.

Now, take a few minutes to do some convincing. Write on the next page, every reason you can think of that will fortify your decision to never smoke again. Be cruel to yourself, call yourself names (stupid, insane, weak, dumb, suicidal, are not bad for starters). Build your resolve, then, read on to learn *how to want to.*

THINKING TIME!
(Last Stop!)

Pretend you were trying to convince someone else not to do something that could possibly kill them. Write down what *you* would tell *them*. You'll probably be surprised at how convincing you can be when helping *someone else*.

_____
_____
_____
_____
_____
_____
_____
_____
_____
_____
_____

**Don't Put Off Until Tomorrow
What You Can Do Today**

NO BUTTS ABOUT IT

HOW TO WANT TO

For whatever personal reasons, you have just decided that you want to avoid having to ask, as Nat King Cole did, "Why me?" Possibly, you have made the most important commitment of your life. You want to stop and need only some added assurance of *how* to *really* want to.

Very possibly, you have already concluded that, with the sizable amount of money you are about to start saving, you can take a vacation or purchase a major appliance or a new wardrobe. One thing you should be certain about: You are now on the road to feeling better about yourself — in so many positive ways.

You know that by staying off the weed, you will actually experience a genuine feeling of pride. Suddenly (it was just a few minutes ago that you were a worried smoker), you no longer have to consider yourself a *problem*.

Think of yourself as having just ended a *crisis* situation. Because it certainly is a crisis situation for anyone who *knows* that he or she is continuing a habit that can kill them or maim them. In short, you have just taken a stiff dose of *common sense!*

But, you are still wondering what you are going to do when you start to get that familiar urge, or when you go to your first cocktail party with all of that temptation. You are going to do whatever it takes to get the job done. Every time you tell yourself to resume smoking, have your new self say, "No thank you!"

You *want* to stop smoking. You already have! And for all the very well known reasons. Well, one way to join the ranks of the reasonable is to agree that, from now on, smoking is no longer an option for you. For you, smoking does not even exist!

You could go to a cocktail party right now and should not be overly apprehensive. Many recommend that you stay away from the things that encourage you to smoke. The all-too familiar advice is to avoid alcohol, coffee, colas and other things that seem to go hand-in-hand with smoking. My advice is to be *reasonable*. Have that martini or cola or cup of coffee. It's too much to expect anyone to give up *everything*. The pressure is too great. By going to that party and having a reasonable number of drinks and *not* smoking, means you have gone *through* the eye of that storm, unharmed, and are a better person for it. It's not what happens at the party that's so important. It's that

NO BUTTS ABOUT IT

super feeling you have on the way home, when you take a deep breath and tell yourself that whatever else you happen to be, you sure as hell are not a smoker. You went to the party, had a rather nice time and didn't smoke.

There's probably never been an ex-smoker who attended a cocktail party without some feeling of apprehension about the *atmosphere* that is so conducive to smoking. (Imagine how a recovering alcoholic feels!) But, these social occasions can be the most rewarding times for you. Bear in mind that about half the people in this country do not smoke. At the party, when you spot a chain smoker after your own heart (and get an urge big enough to choke a horse) casually glance around and spot a non-smoker. The latter is having just as much fun as the smoker, but is not inhaling smoke from a white stick in the process. Do this, and I can guarantee you will be given a good jolt of self respect which will fortify your determination to *remain* a non-smoker. Guarantee: if you have children old enough to know about the harm smoking can do, you have children who will now be extra proud of you.

The reason why I admonished you not to look forward to that very last cigarette *after* completing this book is explained by the headline in small type at the very beginning of this chapter. It truly says it all. "Don't put off until tomorrow, what you can do today." By already having had your last cigarette, you can honestly say, "I've done it!" You are no longer a smoker who wants to stop. You've already *done* it!

Ignoring the advice of that adage explains why most of us never understand the *how* of wanting to do many things. We *want* to lose weight, we *want* to moderate or stop our drinking, or we *want* to give this life of ours a real run for its money, instead of just muddling through. But we do none of these things. We keep putting it off and this is the very reason why we are so often unable to *will* ourselves to apply common sense to our lives.

In his inspirational book, *The Eye of the Storm*, about how to see our way through any severe crisis, Dr. Joe Bishop, for 20 years the pastor of the Presbyterian Church of Rye, New York, put his finger on how to do what must be done. (Joe is now an Episcopalian minister in Rhode Island. His *retirement*, thus far, has been *very* active.)

Joe wrote his book in an effort to explain how he, a man of the church, came to grips with devastating personal tragedy. In rapid succession he lost a teenage son in an automobile accident, and his wife to long-term ravages of cancer. He concluded that his options were limited, indeed. He could have given up and retreated into bitterness and self-defeating pity. Or, he could go forward and, by plunging smack into the middle of the eye of his personal storm, get through it. In short, Joe decided to meet his crisis head-on and, by plowing through it, come out of it positively, with a new understanding and inner serenity that could enable him to accept the harshness of the question: "Why not?"

At this instant, *you* are going through the eye of your personal storm. It has already occurred to you that, by telling yourself that you have had your last cigarette, you are about to face challenges too great to meet successfully.

This is understandable. But what would your reaction be if you saw a child drowning, or if a fire started in your house? You would not hesitate to do whatever was necessary to save that life or to fight that fire. You would, in sum, rise to the occasion.

If you agree that you would react that way, how can you possibly hang your head in the posture of a true weakling and tell yourself that you can't get through *meaningless* pressure that could prompt you to smoke another cigarette?

I recently came across an explanation for this inability to do things we actually want to do very much. It helps explain why we all fail — why, incredibly, we fail to do something when we truly want to do it. I believe that whatever your religious persuasion, you will agree that this is one of the best explanations you have ever come across to explain why you smoked all those years — when you really didn't want to at all. It certainly did the trick for me!

WHY YOU STUMBLE

Do you know the reason for all your stumbling?

Do you know why you have doubts as you walk
Along the way of goodness?

Are you aware of the reason for you being among
Those who say to the Lord:

Tomorrow we shall begin,

So that tomorrow we may say the same thing
Over again.

NO BUTTS ABOUT IT

If you really want to know and love the Lord,
Now is the time to begin.

When I read that passage, it was as if the clouds had parted and I understood — finally! The many times I resumed smoking after a brief or lengthy cessation, I got past the resultant feelings of guilt and self-disgust very easily because I knew, *tomorrow I shall begin* — again. It is this constant putting off, this never-ending rationalization that it's okay to smoke these 60 cigarettes today because, no problem, *tomorrow* I'm going to stop. And when we have that cigarette, first thing the very next morning, before eating a drop of food, we tell ourselves that, "Everything is cool, because I'm *really* going to stop tomorrow."

These *tomorrows* add up to weeks, months and years. These *tomorrows* enable us to accept our shortness of breath and actual fear of death or crippling illness because, somehow, we're going to wind up okay, because there's always *tomorrow*. There's still time.

Your last *tomorrow* was a few minutes ago. Doesn't that give you an enormous feeling of relief and contentment? Aren't you suddenly proud of yourself? Don't you feel better?

And isn't it a good feeling to know that you have just enormously increased your chances of never having to ask: "Why me?"

And, most importantly, isn't it nice to know that when someone notices that you are no longer smoking and asks: "Why did you stop smoking?" you can look them straight

NO BUTTS ABOUT IT

in the eye and reply: "Why not."

The stumbling is over. You can now go through the eye of any storm that comes your way.

You now know *how to want to*.

AFTERWORD

Since I have been a non-smoker during the last four years, I have become an ardent anti-smokist. I hate smoke-filled rooms, automobiles, or commuter cars. Yes, I can, indeed, avoid the latter (that's what America is all about, right?), but frequently a non-smoking car heading out of Grand Central Station was a smoking car on the way in.

As an ex-smoker, *the* aspect of the habit I miss the least is the occasional pack of dry, stale cigarettes. I got to the point of squeezing a package of cigarettes before paying for them, to satisfy myself that the *coffin nails* within were relatively fresh. My foolproof test was that the package had to be soft and squeezable, not unlike that toilet tissue. A pack that was hard almost certainly had stale cigarettes aboard. The stale cigarette smells like something crawled inside and died and, always, snaps in two when you push down on it to extinguish yet another smoking experience. Frequently, the ash falls off when you try to gently tap the weed in an ashtray.

The biggest joy of it all is that stopping is *behind* me. We're talking mega-euphoria! That fellow I described in the book was, and probably still is, scared out of his wits about the possibility that he might go back to smoking. The tough part is that as soon as you resume smoking, you want to give it up. But it's impossible to stop — after staying off cigarettes for years and being back on for only scant minutes. It is incredible how the habit snaps on like a tick, given the chance.

Hopefully, you have read *No Butts About It* and are feeling just great about being a former smoker. There will be temptations ahead, but that's to be expected. Should you get an urge to do something dumb like opting to be a former former smoker, simply project beyond the single cigarette you're thinking of lighting up and imagine the two-packs-a-day habit and what it will do to you, psychologically and physiologically. There are lots of other things you can do with your life than that. Right?

In Eisenhoweresque fashion, there are times that I have that old familiar surge that courses through my entire body, just like the good old days. It is very much akin to a nicotine surge, almost a physiological craving. I mention this, not to frighten you into a what-the-hell relapse. I tell you about it because I am in control of it — all the way. It just happens. It could be the work of the devil or something metaphysical like that. But I have no fear, for self control is with me. Finally.

I actually enjoy these occasional experiences. While I go about my chores, I recall the years when I would have given into a feeling of "just one cigarette, just for old times's sake." I would have smoked a cigarette and, then, because I had had a few puffs already, I would play the game of having another while I was at it just to get a little more of what I had given up.

Then, later, probably at a party, I would scrounge one and then a few and then try to avoid my wife's gaze of disappointment. Hours later I'd try to avoid my children's gaze the next day when they had their familiar devastated expressions of sheer dismay at my utter failure. This was always short of a living hell. Guilt was rampant! But I was back among the ranks of the heavy smokers.

No more. Never. No Way.

Congratulations to YOU!